Photographs by

Liam Blake

Introduction by **Breandán O hEithir**

Appletree Press

First published by
The Appletree Press Ltd,
7 James Street South, Belfast
BT2 8DL, 1987.

Photographs © Liam Blake, 1987
Text © Breandán O hEithir, 1987

British Library Cataloguing in
Publication Data
Blake, Liam
    Impressions of Galway.
    I. Galway (County)—
    Description and travel—
    Views
    I. Title
    941.7'40824'0222
    DA990.G18

    ISBN 0-86281-194-5

    9 8 7 6 5 4 3 2 1

Printed in Ireland

Introduction

GALWAY, the second largest county in Ireland, contains two contrasting regions. Between the river Shannon and Lough Corrib is a plain of limestone; flat, fertile and chequered by stone walls. This is hunting country, a relic of the Big Houses and those who shared a particular way of life in the great sweep of level land between Tuam and Gort.

The Galway Blazers, so called because once in an excess of conviviality they set fire to a hotel in the town of Birr, still keep that tradition alive. The playwright, M. J. Molloy, has written of the people who lived in the shadow of those Big Houses and in fear of the landlords who inhabited them.

Older traditions have also left their mark in the ruined but still imposing abbeys of Claregalway, Abbeyknockmoy and Kilmacduagh. An even older order is represented by *Cnoc Meadh,* an unobtrusive hill west of Tuam, regarded as the home of the fairy folk of Connacht.

South of a line from Ballinasloe to Galway city lies the heartland of Galway hurling and one of the country's richest repositories of traditional music. The first céilí band was formed in Ballinakill in the 1920s, and in nearby Peterswell a fine memorial stands over the grave of Joe Cooley, one of Ireland's finest accordion players.

Part of the Irish Literary Revival blossomed in the area between Gort, Kinvara and Craughwell. Here Lady Gregory discovered vanishing traditions and a speech that became the speciality of the early Abbey Theatre. It was the echo of the receding Irish language in the English spoken by country people and it got its name from the little village of Kiltartan, near Gort.

The traditions were enshrined in folktales and in the poems and songs composed by poor wandering poets in the Irish language. Chief among them was Anthony Raftery, blind, sharp-tongued and prolific, who is buried in Killeeneen, near Craughwell, and whose statue now stands on the village green alongside the main Dublin to Galway road.

Lady Gregory lived at Coole Park and most of the prominent literary figures of the day came to visit her there. It was customary for visitors to cut their initials on a tree in the walled garden. The tree is preserved, and inside a protective grille can be seen the marks made by George Bernard Shaw, Seán O'Casey, Edward Martyn, George Moore and Douglas Hyde. It will be noted that Yeats alone carved out his surname.

So impressed was he by the area and its lore that he bought an old tower at nearby Ballylee and lived there for periods. It is now preserved as a museum. Coole Park House, unfortunately, is no more; a victim to one of the early acts of official vandalism in the new Irish state.

Galway city is the clasp that connects the fertile plains to the east and the wilderness of moorland and granite rocks, lapped by the Atlantic, to the west. It is often called the Gateway to Connemara and the Capital of the Gaeltacht (the Irish-speaking area of south Connemara) but its oldest title is the Citie of the Tribes.

It was once governed by an assembly of powerful families, known as the Tribes of Galway, and sportswriters still refer to the county hurling and football teams as the Tribesmen, to the bewilderment of the uninitiated.

The city straddles the Corrib river that runs between the lake and the sea. A fine weir marks the lake's descent into the river and the salmon can be viewed from the nearby bridge (and fished from a nearby bank) as they prepare for their ascent.

The river ends its short run to the Atlantic at what was once the thatched fishing village of Claddagh, which gave its name to the distinctive ring: two hands clasping a heart. The famous Claddagh fleet of sailing craft is no more. Only a vast flock of swans remain to cruise the estuary at high tide.

Alone among Irish cities of its size, Galway has preserved almost intact its old commercial centre of narrow, winding streets. On Saturday mornings east and west meet in the market in front of the Church of St Nicholas, where Columbus is reputed to have heard mass before setting out for America. Nearby is the window out of which Mayor Lynch hanged his son, according to another unreliable legend, an act which is supposed to have originated the phrase 'Lynch Law'.

In the market the Irish of Connemara and the English of the city and county to the east mingle easily as vegetables, eggs and poultry are sold to the accompaniment of the traditional patter of praise and disparagement.

Two main roads lead west from Galway: one to the north skirting Lough Corrib and on to Clifden, the other skirting Galway Bay with the three Aran Islands to the south lying like gigantic whales on the surface of the sea. It is possible to have the best of both contrasting worlds by taking a circular route, or by criss-crossing the central moorland of lake and bog where peat is still harvested by hand and transported to the nearest roadway by donkey and panniers.

From the village of Bearna west one penetrates the Gaeltacht, where the signposts now carry the place-names in Irish only. Here only the poet Raftery is remembered in the language he used himself. One may be lucky enough to hear one of his love songs or laments sung by a traditional (sean-nós) singer to a hushed audience in a pub at night.

Between An Spidéal and Casla the villages are strung out like beads on a rosary, some of them straying slightly off the main road towards the distant mountains but not too far. At Casla where the Gaeltacht radio service, Raidió na Gaeltachta, has its headquarters, a turn north leads to Ros Muc where Patrick Pearse's cottage is preserved as a museum, and along the coast to Carna where the Gaeltacht ends.

On this coast the currach, a light framework of wooden laths covered by a sheet of tarred canvas, is still used by lobster fishermen in shallow waters. But like the recently refurbished Connemara hookers, once used to carry peat to the Aran Islands and to Kinvara, the currach is now mostly seen at regattas during the summer months in exciting races between teams from all over Connemara and the Aran Islands.

From Carna the road meanders by the fringes of many deep bays to Clifden, one of the most photographed towns in Ireland. This is the centre for the breeding and sale of that hardy breed of horse the Connemara pony. In August a pony show and races are held here and despite the fact that the Connemara pony is no longer in danger of extinction the prices rise all the time.

Before returning to Galway by the northern route it is worth going to see the striking Abbey of Kylemore. Built as a palace for a wealthy merchant's son, it is now a school run by Benedictine nuns. Further north, by the pretty village of Leenane, is Ireland's only fjord, Killary Harbour, deep and spacious enough, it is said, to contain the entire British fleet at anchor.

The road from Clifden to Galway runs beside the distinctive range of mountains known as the Twelve Pins on to Maam Cross, where one of the last street fairs in Ireland is held once a month. However, the Connemara ponies displayed for sale here are every bit as expensive as those on show in the more rarefied surroundings of the Clifden Show.

Approaching Oughterard, Lough Corrib comes into view. The talk here is of big freshwater fish that did not get away. It is one of the country's greatest centres for lake fishing but the profusion of craft-shops on its eastern outskirts gives it the appearance of a town on the edge of an Indian reservation.

From here on to Galway the traveller can enjoy the company of the Corrib, narrowing from lake to river. It is reputed to contain an island for every day of the year; just like Clew Bay and Lough Erne. It is probably another unreliable rumour but it scarcely takes from the beauty of the shimmering, unpolluted expanse of blue-grey water stretching north as far as the eye can see.

BREANDÁN O hEITHIR

◀ Dawn from Inishbofin

Cottage and geese, Galway ▶

◄ Clifden

Village colours, Clifden

Shop front, Clifden ►

◄ Mouth of the Corrib at
Galway city

The Twelve Pins from ►
Inishbofin

Fishing at the salmon weir,
Galway city

Cathedral and salmon weir, ▶
Galway city

Romanesque doorway,
Clonfert Cathedral

Hookers, Kinvara►

◄Aughnanure Castle,
near Oughterard

Repairing fishing nets,
◀ Roundstone

The Shannon at Portumna ▶

◄After mass on Inisheer,
Aran Islands

In the market place, Clifden

Maam Cross fair ►

◄Clifden races

Thoor Ballylee ►

Currach race (overleaf)►

Kylemore Abbey

Lobster fishing, Inishbofin

◀Recess river

Castle at Kinvara

Boys on Inishmore, Aran ▶
Islands

◄ Tree, Maam valley

Killary Harbour ►

Landscape near
Lough Inagh

Landscape near Recess ►

◄Power lines and mist,
Ballynahinch

Sunset and stone wall, ►
Inishmore, Aran Islands